The Best Project You Will Ever Work On Is Yourself

Gail Eaton-Briggs

Published by Gail Eaton-Briggs

First published in 2022

Copyright © Gail Eaton-Briggs

www.everywhensolutions.com.au

The moral rights of the author have been asserted.

All rights reserved. Except as permitted under the Australian Copyright Act 1968 (for example, a fair dealing for the purposes of study, research, criticism or review). No part of this book may be reproduced, stored in a retrieval system communicated or transmitted in any form or by any means without prior written permission.

All inquiries should be made to the author.

Typeset by BookPOD

Front cover design by Gail Eaton-Briggs and image by Svitlana Kutsyn @_artlana_

ISBN: 978-0-6451157-2-7 (pbk)

A catalogue record for this book is available from the National Library of Australia

Preface

I'm in the business of helping others to be their best selves using my Model of Conscious Grit©.

Our lives are better when we are persistent, tenacious, authentic, resilient, determined; when we set goals, plan, are courageous, and have a positive mindset. When we hold those qualities and use them, I call it 'living in the zone of conscious grit'.

Reading and absorbing motivational words and concepts and repeating affirmations help to keep us thinking positive thoughts and living in that zone. There are over 100 motivational phrases and affirmations in this notebook to help you get into – or stay in the zone of conscious grit.

Many of the phrases and snippets of wisdom shared are from my book **Conscious Grit: from stuck to unstoppable**; some are often used quotes and affirmations that my clients relate to.

To optimize the value of the affirmations, you can:

- Write them down lots of times
- Record them and play back during the day
- Write them down and put them where you will see them regularly
- Repeat one several times – aloud or to yourself
- Repeat in front of a mirror
- Join some together

You will find more information about my Model of Conscious Grit at the end of the notebook.

Here's the key to having the life that you want. 🔑 Take it!

Glossary

Catalyst moment – an event (negative or positive) that challenges or disrupts. Catalyst moments are golden learning moments.

Grit – in the context of my Model of Conscious Grit, grit is the collection of personal traits that are characterised by bravery, spirit, courage, consistency, toughness, tenacity, strength, and passion. It is a positive state – unless it's overdone.

The zone of conscious grit – the zone where an individual is persistent, determined, tenacious, resilient, acting with 'big C' Courage, has a future focus and makes plans.

Tipping point – the key to moving from the zone of unconscious grit to conscious grit.

The zone of unconscious grit – the zone where an individual is persistent, determined, tenacious, resilient, acting with 'little c' courage.

Unexpected crap-hand – a term I've invented to mean an event that happens where:

- there is no obvious fix
- there are life-changing adverse effects
- only you know how bad it is
- someone else is adversely affected
- all your choices affect others
- others won't be happy with your decision
- there are long-term impacts to physical and or mental health.

Unstoppable – whatever that term means for you. It will be different for each of us.

*Decide what it is you want. Write it down.
Make a plan and work on it every single day.*

Have the courage to follow your intuition.

Wishes won't work without a goal and a plan.

Don't look back; you are not going that way.

*Remember why you started.
Make it happen. Shock everyone.*

I am strong. I am ready. I am capable.

My confidence rises with every breath I take.
I can. I will. Watch me.

I accept challenge in the knowledge that I have what it takes to work it out and push through.

I have the courage to do what I need to do to move forward.

Be UNSTOPPABLE – whatever that means to YOU.

*You are building unstoppable momentum
with every step you take.*

Be determined. Don't say 'I don't know'. Say 'I'll find out.'

Be resilient. Don't say 'It's too hard.'
Say 'I am up for a challenge.'

Be curious. Don't say 'I can't.' Say 'How do I learn?'.

Cut the strings of your obsessive and unhelpful thoughts and let them drift away.

A year from now, you will wish you had started today.

*Event plus response equals outcome (E + R = O).
Remember, YOU are in charge of your response.*

*Success comes when you keep on trying
even when there seems no hope at all.*

*If you don't like something, change it or
choose a different attitude to deal with it.*

It is OK to let go of things that no longer bring you joy or serve you well.

Surround yourself with positive people. It is infectious. Rid yourself of emotional vampires. They are also infectious.

I choose to have a good day.

I forgive others. I forgive myself. I release the past. I trust in the present.

I am good enough. Always have been. Always will be.

I'm not afraid of being brave.
I inch myself toward my bravest self.

I replace my feelings of stress, worry and anxiety with calmness and tranquility.

When we are stuck in the zone of Unconscious Grit, we know in our heart of hearts we can't keep going on the way we are. It's time to catch a tipping point.

*Tipping points are out there. They are swirling in the ether.
Be on the look out and when you need one - catch it.*

Tipping Point. The point at which a series of small changes becomes significant enough to cause a large, more meaningful change.

When we find and catch a tipping point, we step through a door that we previously thought was closed.

You know you've caught a tipping point when you feel validated and affirmed.

You know you've caught a tipping point when you feel relief that an uncertain situation is now resolving – because of a small or large step you have taken.

You know you've caught a tipping point when you simultaneously feel a sense of readiness, excitement and trepidation.

You know you've caught a tipping point when you feel peace, comfort, contentment and calm.

You know you've caught a tipping point when you feel like things are (finally) going your way.

In everything you do, YOU are creating YOUR reality and writing YOUR story.

Catalyst moments are gold. They are the launching pad for your future success.

Everything you have been through has been building your beautiful resilience muscles.

Courage is like a muscle. We strengthen it by using it.

Are you fighting a battle that doesn't matter. Stop.

The bad news is time flies.
The good news is that you are the pilot.

Tomorrow is perfect when it arrives and puts itself in our hands. Honour it.

*You know you've caught a tipping point
when you feel a sudden spike of satisfaction
due to something good happening.*

You know you've caught a tipping point when you feel a sense of optimism and anticipation that the future will be positive.

You know you've caught a tipping point when for an unexplainable reason you feel inspired, engaged, uplifted and motivated.

You know you've caught a tipping point when you experience a feeling of curiosity that demands and captures your attention.

You know you've caught a tipping point when you don't know why, but your heart sings.

I'm happy with what I have while working for what I want.

I'm proud of myself for getting this far.

I choose calm over every other emotion that stirs me up.

I breathe in. I breathe out. I am ready to act today.

You can't drive a parked car, so find some courage and drive into the zone of Conscious Grit.

Conscious Grit is a special kind of grit.

Think like a bee. Hover in the zone of Conscious Grit.

If you choose to stay in the zone of Unconscious Grit, you might be missing out on a better life. It's that simple.

Gritty (verb). Being gritty is good.

In the zone of Conscious Grit, goals are important.

Qualities of Conscious Grit: Generous. Reflective. Intrepid. Tactful.

*Qualities of Conscious Grit: Goal setter.
Resourceful. Intuitive. Tenacious.*

*Qualities of Conscious Grit: Grateful.
Resilient. Intentional. Thoughtful.*

*Qualities of Conscious Grit: Grounded.
Rational. Insightful. Trusty.*

*Qualities of Conscious Grit: Good hearted.
Resilient. Inspired. Teachable.*

When you have Conscious Grit, you cannot be Gossipy, Resentful, Ignorant, Temperamental.

Your time as a caterpillar has expired.
Your wings are ready.

Challenge your stories and reframe them into helpful truths that help not hinder you.

When your values and behaviours align, you will feel so much better.

Your mind will always believe what you tell it. Feed it with positivity.

Living 'like a boss' means living with a 'stylish confidence'.

Limiting beliefs are false beliefs we have about ourself. They hold us back. We need to figure out what they are and deal with them.

*Be the reason someone smiles today.
And don't forget you are someone too.*

We all mess up. When you do, fess up and fix up.

Instead of 'I'm sorry I'm late', say 'thank you for waiting'.

*Instead of 'I'm sorry for talking so much,'
say 'thank you for listening'.*

Instead of 'I'm sorry for being so upset', say 'thank you for being patient'.

Instead of 'I'm sorry I need help', say 'thank you for helping'.

When you have big C Courage, you stretch yourself and stick with it, even when things are not going well. You persist.

Those who have grit and courage and use them wisely are to be admired.

Minimise your contact with negative people; rid yourself of emotional vampires.

One unexpected crap hand does not determine the book of your life.

You can be the person you want to be.
Your future is in your hands.

*Take a deep breath. You CAN do it.
You've got this my friend.*

Whether you think you can or you can't – you are right.

When a fruit tree doesn't fruit, you fix the environment in which it grows; not the fruit.

Choose to focus on experiences and people that are life sustaining, not life draining.

Anxiety and worry will not change the past; your time and energy are best invested in the present moment.

Don't say, 'I'm worried I'll fall.' Instead say, 'If I fall, I'll get back up.'

Don't say, 'I'm not good at it'. Instead say, 'I can get better'.

*Don't say, 'I need to know everything'.
Instead say, 'I don't need to know everything,
and I'll find out more as I go along.'*

When you accept yesterday for what it was, it will trouble you no more.

If you get tired, learn to rest, not to quit.

Is your self-care at the top of your to do list?
There is only one right answer.

Listen to your intuition and what it's telling you; it is your inner voice of wisdom.

Create your own 'kitchen cabinet', your own 'tribe'. These are the people who will help you and support you with no judgement.

Lead effectively by managing self, managing up, managing down and managing sideways. SUDS©

Know yourself, own yourself and be yourself.

Know your boundaries and let others know what is OK for you and what isn't.

Life is way too short to spend another day at war with yourself.

It's a good day when you realise you are the one that's been holding you back the whole time.

When you realise you really don't know as much as you think you know, you listen more.

Thinking the same thoughts over and over again won't actually change anything. It just flattens your battery.

What did you learn today? What did you do that taught you something. What will you do next time?

You can choose how you respond to any situation, but you cannot control the reactions of others.

We always have a choice.
We choose our actions and our mindset.

If you have to compare your current self with someone, make sure it's your previous self and no one else.

*Learning about yourself never ends.
It's a bit like peeling an onion.*

Unstuck? Live in the zone of Conscious Grit and be unstoppable.

Where to next?

The Model of Conscious Grit©

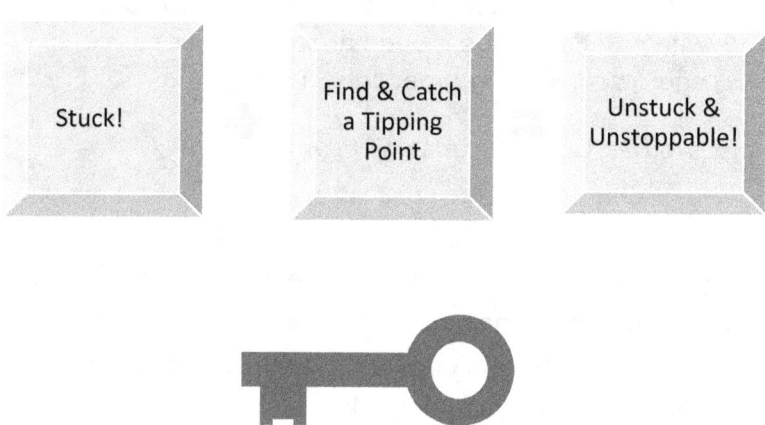

My Model of Conscious Grit is helping many get unstuck and find new directions in their personal and professional lives.

Case study

Toward the end of 2021 M enrolled in the Model of Conscious Grit 30 day Challenge. She had been feeling stuck in her professional life. M knew she wanted to do something different but couldn't see a clear path.

M completed the challenge, focusing on using big C Courage; in her coaching session, we talked through how she could apply a range of tools to her situation.

M booked another coaching session 5 weeks later.

> So many things had changed in that period
> - a successful job application
> - a successful interview
> - she had landed the job that she had aspired to for years
> - resigned and accepted the role
> - is also actively laying the foundations for the future with practical steps around another of her passions
> - energised, looking great, lots of smiles!
>
> Her words: "Gail, I'm not stuck anymore".

I can't guarantee that will be your experience - but I can tell you M's story and encourage you to use the Model of Conscious Grit to tackle your own challenges, obstacles, circumstances and create your new story. M took the key.

Over the page you can find the Introduction from my book Conscious Grit: from stuck to unstoppable. You can:

- read the book available at https://www.amazon.com.au/Conscious-Grit-unstoppable-Gail-Eaton-Briggs/dp/0645115703
- do a 30-Day Challenge to get you from stuck to unstoppable
- book me for keynotes, presentations and workshops
- book me for coaching 1-1

Contact me:

Gail@everywhensolutions.com.au

I answer all enquiries personally.

And in closing, I can't resist a final opportunity to help you be your best self, so here's a call to action for you — what will you do today that your future self will thank you for?

Take care!

Gail

Introduction

Sometimes I lie awake at night and ask, 'Where have I gone wrong?' And then a voice says to me 'This is going to take more than one night.'

— Charlie Brown, *Peanuts*

If you are having thoughts like Charlie Brown, this book will help you.

I use the story of being dealt an 'unexpected crap-hand' when I was 22 to show you how I was able to keep my kids safe and then create a good life. I became unstoppable.

We all have our own definition of what 'unstoppable' means. For me, once I started to get momentum through living in the zone of conscious grit, I found that opportunities opened up to me, and I had confidence to grab them and create more pathways to enrich my life. I have lots to share with you with the aim that you will be a step ahead of me. You'll know the traps and pitfalls. You'll have information that I didn't have at the time I needed it. You will see that it's possible to get unstuck and be unstoppable.

There are three parts to the story that I want to share with you.

Part One is my story and how it inspired me to create a model that others can use and benefit from. I'll tell you more about grit and how to get into the zone that will help you most – the zone of conscious grit. You'll find this in Chapters One to Three.

Part Two gives you all the information and knowledge that I now know but didn't know then. You'll find this in Chapters Four to Seven.

Part Three gives you many capabilities that you can add into your life in conscious grit. These are the skills and tools that I've learned over the years. I've chosen those that have been most impactful in all areas of my life. You can use them in the workplace, with your family, in good times, and when you need to fix up a mess. You'll find this in Chapters Eight to Ten.

'Grit' is a word that people have different opinions about.

When I think that someone's 'gritty' I see it as a good thing. My model, though, challenges the assumption that all grit is equally good; I say there is grit and there is even better grit.

There are some people who associate the trait of 'grit' with aggressive, achieve-at-all-costs, tread-on-other-people behaviour. This book is not about that type of grit.

I'm grateful for my grit. I have it in spades and have needed it repeatedly in my life through various personal and professional challenges. In talking to and observing others over the years, I've seen many examples of people with grit. I admire those people who have grit and use it wisely.

I have designed a model that helps individuals, who are already gritty, understand why they are stuck. I define this state as being in the 'zone of unconscious grit'.

In the zone of unconscious grit, you are trying hard by using your powers of persistence, determination, tenacity, 'little c' courage and resilience. There is no shame in being in this zone – but it's hard work and progress is limited.

There is another state of being: it's when you are living in the zone of conscious grit. Here, individuals combine tenacity, determination, persistence, 'big C' Courage and resilience with a focus on the future and a commitment to planning.

It's never too late to move into the zone of conscious grit. I was in the zone of unconscious grit for nearly five years. I was stuck.

Getting to the zone of conscious grit might be elusive. You need to find and catch a tipping point. It can be done, and I will tell you how I did it.

In this book you'll find models to guide you, words to motivate you, personal projects to do, information from researchers, and tips and tools that I've used.

By the end of the book, you'll be able to say with confidence, 'I don't deal the cards. I play the ones I'm given, and I do it really well.'

You will also say, 'I was stuck, now I'm unstoppable.'

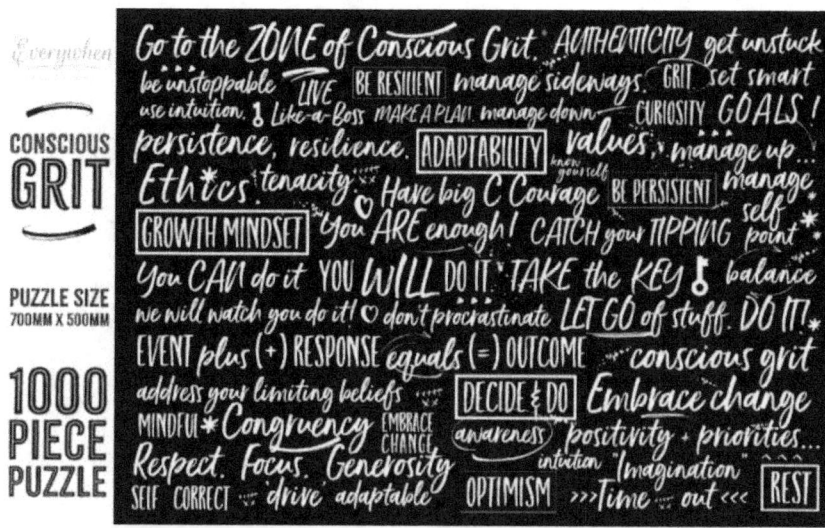

Available from https://www.everywhensolutions.com.au/shop/

Or email gail@everywhensolutions.com.au

www.ingramcontent.com/pod-product-compliance
Lightning Source LLC
Chambersburg PA
CBHW051425290426
44109CB00016B/1442